# Rocks, Crystals, and Gems

Date of Manufacture: January 2016
Manufactured by: Toppan Leefung Printing Co, Ltd., Shenzhen, China

9 8 7 6 5 4 3 2 1

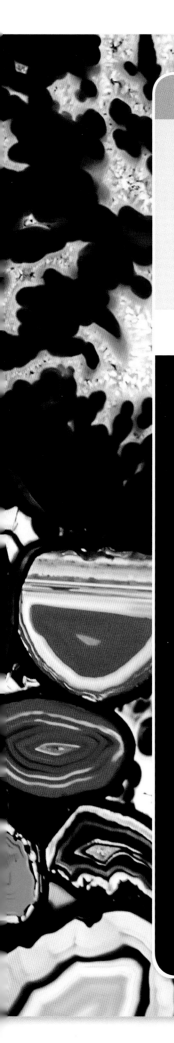

# Introduction

There is no such thing as an ordinary rock. Every rock has been on an amazing, often violent, journey from deep inside the Earth to the surface and back to the depths again. A journey that took millions, even billions of years, and along the way turned carbon to diamond, limestone to marble, and organisms to coal. Rocks provide us with minerals, metals, fuels, building materials, gems, and so much more. You will never take a rock for granted ever again.

# Contents

**Read on to discover Earth's deepest and most colorful secrets...**

# A world of rocks

Rocks tell the **history** of the Earth and rocks will provide the materials to build Earth's future and our **future**. The planet's outer **layers** are made of rock, and humankind has used this resource throughout history. In the **Stone Age**, rocks were used for shelter, **weapons**, and even the pigments for cave paintings. The Copper, Bronze, and **Iron ages** are so named because that is when humans learned to extract **minerals** from rocks to make metal **tools**, weapons, utensils, and ornamental objects. Even in the **Space Age**, rocks and minerals provide essential resources.

## Facts and figures

**Metals in rocks**

These metals are found in rocks in the Earth's crust. Rocks that contain metals are called ores.

**Metal: Gold**
**Ore: Native gold**
This soft valuable metal is used in computers, jewelry, and even spacesuit visors!

**Metal: Silver**
**Ore: Acanthite**
Once used to make coins, silver is found in jewelry, solar panels, and medical dressings.

**Metal: Platinum**
**Ore: Sperrylite**
This gray-white metal, often valued above gold, is used in jewelry and catalytic converters for vehicles.

**Metal: Uranium**
**Ore: Uraninite**
This is used in nuclear fission, which has applications in power generation, weapons, and medicine.

## The Earth is at least 4.4 billion years old!

The Danxia Landform in China has multicolored ridges made from red sandstone and mineral deposits

## What's petrology?

Petrology is the study of the origin and composition of rocks. It is a branch of geology, which is the study of Earth's structure.

## Hard and soft rocks

The minerals in a rock will cause it to be "hard" or "soft" and resistant or not to water. Hard rocks are often metamorphic or igneous, while soft rocks are usually sedimentary.

## Did you know?

The oldest rocks on Earth are meteorites that formed in space before crashing on Earth. The Hoba Meteorite in Namibia, Africa, is the largest meteorite so far discovered.

Quartzite is a hard metamorphic rock

Sunstone is an orange colored feldspar

## What is a rock...

A rock is naturally formed from a mixture of one or more minerals that have clumped together into a solid lump. Quartzite rock consists of one mineral (quartz) while granite is a mixture of 11 minerals. Rocks of the same type will look and feel different depending on where they were formed and how they were formed.

## and a mineral?

A mineral has a fixed composition and a uniform structure. It forms naturally from inorganic (not plant or animal) materials. Over 4,900 minerals have been discovered. Feldspar is a mineral found in 60 per cent of rocks. Gems are mineral crystals.

## What is a crystal?

A crystal is a mineral that forms into a particular shape. This is because its atoms are arranged in a three-dimensional, geometric pattern. This gives a crystal its flat faces, sharp angles, and shape. Amethyst – purple crystals of the mineral quartz – form squat or tall pyramid-shaped crystals.

Squat pyramid-shaped amethyst crystals

## Fact file

### Types of rocks

The three rock types are grouped according to how they were made. Pressure, heat, and location create a rock's grain size, texture, and mineral content.

**Igneous rocks**
These rocks form from liquid magma that has erupted and cooled slowly or quickly. Gabbro is a slow-cooled igneous rock.

**Metamorphic rocks**
Intense heat and/or pressure changes a rock into another type of rock. Slate is formed when clay or volcanic ash change.

**Sedimentary rocks**
These form when sediments of eroded rocks are compressed under water. Limestone sediment forms chalkboard chalk.

# Recycling rocks

Rocks do not stay the same forever. They undergo **changes** due to weathering, **erosion**, earthquakes, and volcanoes. This process is called the **rock cycle**. Igneous rocks below Earth's surface create uplifts to form mountains. **Weathering** slowly breaks down mountains into fragments and sediments. **Erosion** carries the fragments and sediments away and **deposits** them, often into water, where they are compressed into sedimentary rocks. When exposed to **heat** and **pressure**, sedimentary rocks become metamorphic rocks, which can be heated again to form **magma** and igneous rocks.

## Boulder to pebble

Rain, wind, waves, ice, salt, plants, and animals cause rocks, even the hardest ones, to weather (wear away) – boulders become pebbles, and mountains become hills.

## Earth movers

Earthquakes are caused by volcanoes and the movement of tectonic plates, which causes rock masses to break and the ground to move.

Waves erode rocks along Big Sur, California, USA

## Did you know?

Seismologists measure the waves of energy that are produced in an earthquake. The seismic waves are the blue lines, and the globe shows the earthquake's location.

The **Earth** is in **continual** change, always **weathering** and **reforming**.

Lava-formed black obsidian, Rainbow Mountains, Iceland

## Magma on the move

Magma, which consists of liquid mantle rocks, minerals, and gases from deep inside the Earth, collects in chambers. If the pressure becomes too great, an eruption will occur. Some magma will escape into vents to cool slowly; some escapes to the surface as lava in a volcanic eruption.

## Fact file

### Inside the Earth

If you sliced through the Earth as though it was an onion, you would see the layers within. Rocks on the surface reveal what's happened far below.

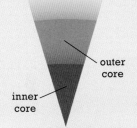

crust
upper mantle
lower mantle
outer core
inner core

## What's erosion?

Erosion is the process by which weathered rock fragments and sediments are moved to another place by wind, water, ice, and gravity. When the transported sediments settle, it is called deposition. Monument Valley, Utah, was created from Rocky Mountain erosion that was deposited and cemented into sandstone. The sandstone weathered into towering formations.

## Lithification

The process of turning deposited sediments into rock is called lithification. Fine sediments, like clay, become slate mostly due to compression, but larger sediments are bonded together by dissolved minerals.

Natural forces continue to shape Monument Valley, USA

### Crust

This is the outermost layer of solid rock on which we live. It consists of 10 major tectonic plates.

### Mantle

The upper layer of the mantle is solid rock, while the lower layer is semi-molten rock (magma).

### Outer core

Surrounding the inner core, this is an extremely hot layer of liquid iron, nickel, and other elements.

### Inner core

At the center is a solid core of iron and nickel. Its high temperature makes it the "engine room" of the Earth.

Lithified rocks at Culm Measures, Cornwall, UK

# Hot rocks

**Igneous** rocks are, without a doubt, Earth's rock stars! They are formed from **molten** rock that forces its way through cracks and fractures to either **erupt** onto the Earth's surface or collect in **chambers** underground. Molten rocks that cool quickly on the surface have tiny **crystals** and are called extrusive igneous rocks. Those that **cool** slowly in chambers form larger crystals and are called **intrusive** igneous rocks. All 700 types of igneous rocks are made of the same eight **elements** that have melted to form the **silicate** minerals found in 90 percent of the Earth's crust.

## Volcanoes release pressure that builds up in the mantle and core.

## Facts and figures

### Violent volcanoes

**Indonesia**
Since 1600, multiple volcanic eruptions in Indonesia have caused the deaths of over 160,000 people.

**Iceland**
When Laki, Iceland, erupted in 1783, it spewed noxious gases and lava for eight months. More than 20 percent of the population died of famine and disease.

**South America**
Nevado del Ruiz, Columbia, erupted in 1985 and ejected a molten mass of rock and gas that melted a glacier. It was the glacier and mudslides that caused so much death and destruction.

**Caribbean**
A pyroclastic flow – a fast-moving liquid mass of rock and gas – from Mount Pelée volcano reached a temperature of 1,967°F (1,075°C).

Lava shoots hundreds of feet above Mount Etna in Sicily, Italy, during an eruption in 2013

## Did you know?

Pumice is an igneous rock that is peppered with holes. The holes are formed by bubbles of gas trapped in the magma as it rapidly cools. Pumice is so light it can float on water.

## Black sand

When lava flows into water, it cools super quickly and shatters into sand-like fragments. When the flow is large enough, a black sand beach will be formed.

## New landforms

The material that erupts from volcanoes changes existing landforms and creates new landforms.

# Volcanic islands

Since 1918, 19 islands have formed after eruptions. Niijima appeared in November 2013 after an undersea volcanic eruption off Nishimo Shima Island, Japan. The crater rose above sea level and continuing eruptions caused the growing new island to merge with the older island to the south.

Niijima has merged with the nearby older island

Basalt columns formed by lava in the Czech Republic

An abandoned tin mine in Cornwall, UK made from granite

## Basalt

Basalt is a dark, fine-grained igneous rock that contains iron and magnesium and other minerals, like quartz. Some basalts form deep in the Earth, others cool on the surface. It is abundant on Earth and on the Moon. This rock is used in construction and as ballast under railway tracks.

## Granite

This important rock contains quartz, feldspars and other minerals and it can be red, pink, gray, or white in color. It is an intrusive igneous rock that cooled slowly. It is a very hard rock and is used in construction. The King's Tomb (2580 BCE) at Giza, Egypt, is made of red granite.

# Fact file

## Other igneous rocks

Igneous rocks dominate Earth's upper layers and many, like granite, are common. Here are three lesser-known igneous rocks.

**Pele's hair**
When the wind catches strands of lava thrown into the air during an eruption, they form a volcanic glass called Pele's hair.

**Ignimbrite**
Consisting mostly of pumice, this pink-gray rock is formed when layers of volcanic rock and gas are compressed and cooled.

**Peridotite**
This olive-green rock is mined for its valuable chromium. Kimberlite, a variety of peridotite, often contains diamonds.

# Rocks that change

Metamorphism is the process by which a rock **changes** its appearance and **structure**. This happens when a rock is exposed to **heat** and pressure. Any rock – igneous, sedimentary, and even **metamorphic** – can be changed into another type of rock. Heat and pressure **transform** limestone into marble, shale or mudstone into slate, and **sandstone** into quartzite. Metamorphism can occur at different **depths** and with varying amounts of heat and **pressure**. Uplift and erosion bring metamorphic rocks to the Earth's **surface**.

## Facts and figures

### Types of layering

**Foliated rock**
The thin layers form under high pressure where pressure in one direction is greater than in any other direction. This gives rocks like slate and gneiss a striped appearance.

**Non-foliated rock**
A dense, uniform rock without layers, like marble and quartzite, forms under low, even amounts of pressure.

### Types of metamorphosis

**Contact**
This happens when magma bakes surrounding rocks.

**Regional**
When heat and pressure affect a large area, like a mountain, the entire formation changes.

**Dynamic**
When rocks rub against each other, a powder forms that is changed by heat and pressure.

## Did you know?

About 48 million sq ft (4.5 million sq m) of white marble was used on the exterior of 543 buildings in Ashgabat, Turkmenistan. It set a Guinness World Record.

The Taj Mahal, India, is covered with translucent white marble

**Marble cuts clean in any direction, so it is perfect for sculpture and construction.**

## Marble damage

Though marble is a dense, heavy rock, lemon juice, vinegar, and wine can etch into its surface. Many ancient marble sculptures have been badly damaged by acid rain and pollution.

## Just add minerals

If minerals are present in the limestone, the marble will be colored. Serpentine creates green marble, and iron will make it red.

Naturally occurring layers of slate

**Other examples**

Even though rocks are under intense heat and pressure, they don't melt during metamorphosis. If the rock melted, it would form an igneous rock.

**Schist**
This regional metamorphic rock will split into layers, and the sample above contains shiny flat flakes of the mineral mica.

## Slate

This is formed when sedimentary rocks like mudstone or shale are affected by low-grade heat and pressure that cause the minerals to align at right angles to the direction of greatest pressure. This creates layers that split cleanly leaving smooth, flat surfaces. This makes slate perfect for roof tiles and pool tables! Slate can metamorphose under different conditions into schist and gneiss.

## Eclogite

Eclogite is one of the rarest metamorphic rocks and is formed under heat and pressure 30 miles (50 km) below the Earth's surface. This rock, made of gabbro and basalt, can contain red garnets and diamonds.

Eclogite with red garnet and green omphacite-jade crystals

**Anthracite**
Also known as smokeless coal or black diamond, anthracite is regionally metamorphosed coal. It is 91–98 percent carbon.

## Granite to gneiss

When granite or mudstone is subjected to high-grade heat and pressure, gneiss forms. Though gneiss displays layers of different minerals, it will not split cleanly like slate. Gneiss found in Canada is more than 4.03 billion years old, making it the oldest rock to be discovered on the Earth's crust.

Canadian gneiss with layers of pink granite and a darker iron-rich rock

**Quartzite**
When quartz sandstone is affected by high heat and pressure, quartzite will be formed. Quartzite is a hard-wearing rock.

# Layer upon layer

Sedimentary rock is made from **igneous**, metamorphic, and other sedimentary rocks. The weathered **sediments** of these rocks are carried away by **wind**, water or ice, or earthquakes and deposited, usually in **layers** under water, and then compacted. The layers often include decayed **plants** and dead animals. Some sedimentary rocks are fine-grained, like **chert**; others, like conglomerate, contain small stones and **shells**. Dissolved minerals **cement** the sediments together. Some sedimentary rocks found in **Greenland** are 3.9 billion years old!

## Facts and figures

**How do we use sedimentary rocks?**

**Bauxite**
The ore from which aluminum is extracted.

**Conglomerate**
This rock is crushed for use in the construction industry.

**Dolomite**
Can be used as a soil conditioner, in livestock feed and in the making of glass, ceramics, bricks and chemicals.

**Flint**
Used as fire-starters and building material.

**Iron ore**
Used to make steel.

**Pumice**
An abrasive used in soaps and nail files.

**Quartz sand**
Used to make glass.

**Shale**
Source of liquid and gaseous hydrocarbons (fuel).

## What's CaCO₃?

This is the symbol for calcium carbonate – chalk. Chalk forms under water from calcite shells. It is soft enough to write with, but hard enough to form the White Cliffs of Dover, UK.

## Rock cycle

When a soft sedimentary rock like shale is affected by heat and pressure, it changes to slate, which is a harder metamorphic rock.

A "marble cake" of colored sandstones at White Pocket, Arizona, USA

## Did you know?

Uluru in Australia's Northern Territory was formed 550 million years ago under a sea, but now rises 1,140 feet (348 m) above the ground. Millennia of weathering has shaped this monolith.

The rose-red Treasury (Al Khazneh) building at Petra, Jordan

## Red sandstone

This sandstone, often called Nubian sandstone, is found in northeastern Africa, and is the rock into which the city of Petra was carved over 2,000 years ago. It is red or brown, but can exhibit a rainbow of colors. Sandstone is crushed to make building sand, cut into blocks, carved for sculpture and ground for glass production.

## Coal

This fossil fuel was formed 300 million years ago from dead plant matter that was compacted to form peat and eventually coal. Coal is mostly carbon, and has been burned to provide heat since 2000 BCE. Coal is a non-renewable resource.

As **rings** in a **tree** tell its **story,** **layers** of **rock** **reveal** Earth's timeline.

Peat is cut into blocks and dried for use as fuel in Ireland

### Which minerals?

Sedimentary rocks contain quartz, clay, and calcite and at times iron oxide, feldspar and mica minerals.

### On the surface

Sedimentary rocks make up 75 percent of rocks on the Earth's surface. But 10 miles (16 km) below the surface accounts for only five percent.

## Sun-dried evaporites

These form when a liquid containing dissolved chemical sediments dries up (evaporate) under the sun's heat. Halite, or rock salt, is an evaporite. It is normally white, but impurities will color it. More than just a food flavoring and road de-icer, salt has 14,000 other industrial uses.

Either impurities or a bacteria turned this rock salt orange

# Stories in stone

**Fossils** are the remains or imprints of animals and plants that lived **thousands** to billions of years ago. The hardest parts of the animal, like **bone** and shell, have the greatest chance of surviving as fossils. But whether it is a fossil of a **paw** print (a trace fossil) or a complete **skeleton**, it opens a window on Earth's history. Fossils have been found on every **continent** on Earth, mostly in sedimentary rock. The most recently **uncovered** fossil hotspot is in Liaoning Province, China, where **paleontologists** have discovered fossils of five feathered **dinosaur** species.

## Facts and figures

**Latin word**
Fossil is a Latin word meaning "dug up."

**Fireball!**
Without fossils, we would never have known about dinosaurs, and why they perished 65 million years ago. In the rocks where dinosaur fossils have been found, there is evidence of a fireball and suffocating dust clouds that were caused by an asteroid hitting Earth.

**No bone**
Fossil bone does not contain bone, only the minerals that replaced it during fossilization.

**The oldest dinosaur**
A 230 million-year-old prosauropod fossil was found in Madagascar, off Africa.

**The largest dinosaur**
A sauroposeidon fossil showed this species was 59 feet (18 m) tall and weighed as much as nine elephants.

Fossil of a marine reptile (ichthyosaur) from the Jurassic period, 201–145 million years ago

**There is a one in a million chance of an animal fossilizing.**

## Stone or bone?

Stones are often mistaken for bone fossils. A stone will look the same inside and outside, whereas the inside of a bone fossil contains channels and tiny holes.

## Ancient dung

Coprolites are fossilized animal dung, and they reveal what animals were eating. Coprolites are rare as poop decays quickly.

## Did you know?

The oldest fossils are 3.2 billion-year-old algae. Layers of algae build up to form mounds called stromatolites. This stromatolite in Western Australia is 3,000 years old and still growing!

# Mary Anning

Born in 1799 in a seaside town in Dorset, UK, Mary taught herself about geology. She found the first complete marine reptile fossil on what is now called the Jurassic Coast. To earn money, Anning's family sold the fossils that Mary collected from a table set up at a coach stop on the beach.

# Fossilized plants

Plant fossils provide information about Earth's history. Fossils indicate that Antarctica, for example, was once thickly carpeted with rainforest, and rocks from Greenland show evidence of global warming over 200 million years ago! Coal and oil were formed by fossilized plants.

Trilobite fossils like the ones that Anning found and sold

Fossilized leaves and stem of a plant, possibly a seaweed

## Preserved in amber

All trees produce a resin, and when the resin is fossilized it is called amber. Since Neolithic times (starting 10,200 BCE) amber has been prized as a gemstone, but to fossil hunters it is prized for the animals and plants that were trapped and preserved in the resin.

Flies and a bee preserved in two amber gems

# Fact file
## Fossil formation

**Stage one**
Fossilization can occur if an animal dies in sand, mud, or water, the corpse is not scavenged, and the temperature is very low.

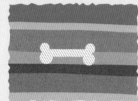

**Stage two**
The corpse is covered by sediment that will slow but not stop skin and organs decaying. Bones and shells are more resilient.

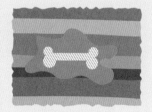

**Stage three**
Layers of sediment compress over the corpse and form rock. Minerals soak down to preserve or dissolve the skeleton.

**Stage four**
The rock weathers, exposing the preserved skeleton, a mineral mold of the skeleton or an imprint of the skeleton.

# Remarkable rocks

Our planet contains an array of **amazing** rock formations. Some are even **hidden** beneath our feet! These beautiful caverns, etched over **millennia** by slightly acidic water seeping through **limestone**, are otherworldly and strange. Then there are those places where natural **forces** have carved rock into fantastical shapes, created **multi-colored** landscapes or **chasms** so deep that they seem bottomless. But while we gaze at these wonders that appear **permanent** but aren't, Earth is constantly making and **transforming** rocks.

## Facts and figures

**Highest elevation**
When the Indian tectonic plate pushed against the Asian plate, they formed Mount Everest, which continues growing 25 mm each year.

**Lowest elevation**
The Dead Sea is 1,300 ft (400 m) below sea level and was formed when two tectonic plates spread apart causing a "dip" in the crust.

**Deepest gorge**
As plates forced the Himalayas higher, a river sliced through the uplift creating Kali Gandaki Gorge. This gorge sits 3.4 miles (5,500 m) below the surrounding peaks.

**Deepest trench**
At 6.8 miles (10,994 m) below sea level lies Challenger Deep in the Mariana Trench. This trench was created when a tectonic plate curved down as it pushed up against another tectonic plate.

## Did you know?

Limestone formations caused by dripping water are known as dripstones. A column is formed when the lowest tip of a stalactite meets the topmost tip of a stalagmite.

Jeita Caves, Lebanon, has a world-record stalactite that hangs 26 ft (8.2 m) from the cave roof

## Illegal trade

Growing less than 4 inches (10 cm) in 1,000 years, it is illegal in most countries to collect, mine, or sell stalagmites and stalactites.

## Drip by drip

When water drips into a cave, each drip leaves a tiny amount of mineral (calcite) on the cave roof. These form into stalactites. When drips hit the floor, the minerals build a stalagmite.

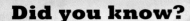

**Stalactites and stalagmites are sometimes referred to collectively as dripstone.**

Troll's Tongue with a glacial valley in the background

## Fact file

### Nature's rock sculptures

The forces that shape the Earth are movement of the tectonic plates, volcanic eruptions, weathering, erosion, and deposition.

**Ball's Pyramid**

The world's tallest stack, off Australia in the Pacific Ocean, is 1,800 ft (551 m) high. Only 0.5 percent of the original volcano remains.

**Pancake Rocks**

These formations in New Zealand are the weathered remains of compressed limestone separated by layers of softer mud.

**Nakalele Blowhole**

This Hawaiian blowhole formed when waves wore a hole in a cave roof. When a wave enters the cave, it blasts up through the hole.

# Troll's Tongue

Jutting almost 2,300 ft (700 m) above a glacial valley in Norway, this narrow horizontal rock shelf was created when water from an Ice Age glacier froze and expanded in cracks in the mountain. This eventually caused a huge chunk of gneiss rock to break off, leaving behind what the Norwegian locals call Trolltunga.

Some formations in the Shilin Stone Forest are 100 ft (30 m) tall

# Stone forest

The Shilin Stone Forest area was a vast expanse of sea about 270 million years ago, but movement of the tectonic plates caused an uplift that forced the water to retreat. The exposed limestone weathered over millions of years to create these amazing formations, some of which resemble animals, trees, and humans.

# The Wave

The colorful U-shaped troughs were formed by water carving deeper and deeper into the sandstone during the Jurassic Age. When the water stopped flowing, wind continued to weather and shape this extraordinary place in Arizona, USA.

The Wave is an unmarked path in the middle of a hot wilderness

# Hard-working rocks

Humans have used rocks since **ancient** times for buildings, tools, jewelery, and **sculpture**. Rocks have also been used in dyes, **medicines**, cosmetics, and even evil deeds! Ancient Egyptians sprinkled coffins with **hematite** to make any grave robbers sneeze. Persians knew that **arsenic** was a powerful poison. Minerals are in almost everything we **use** and consume. All these valuable **resources** are extracted from inside the Earth. It is estimated that 24 tons (22,000 kg) of rocks and **minerals** are required **annually** to meet the needs of one American citizen.

## Facts and figures

**Useful rocks and minerals**

Every day, we use or consume things that are made using rocks or minerals.

| | |
|---|---|
| **Batteries:** lead, lithium | **Mirror:** silver |
| **Bike handlebars:** zinc (used to make chrome) | **Pencils:** graphite |
| | **Plastic bottle:** crude oil |
| **Cat litter:** zeolites | **Sandwich bread:** trona (baking soda) |
| **Computer chips:** silica | |
| **Soda can:** bauxite | **Shoes:** chromite (used in tanning) |
| **Fireworks:** sulphur | |
| **Fizzy drinks:** phosphate | **Sparkly make up:** mica |
| **Jeans:** pumice (to distress the denim) | **Coffee mug:** clay |
| | **Toothpaste:** fluorite, pumice, kaolinite, titanium |
| **Light bulbs:** tungsten, molybdenite | |

## Eroding the Earth

Mining for rocks and minerals moves more earth than erosion. To make one ton of copper, over 137 tons of copper ore are dug out of the ground.

## Non-renewable

Minerals are non-renewable resources because they take millions of years to form and can't be replaced during a person's life.

**Easter Island's ancient statues, called moai, are made from volcanic tuff.**

Layers of sediment have left only the heads of the moai exposed

## Did you know?

Iron-rich lodestones are magnetic rocks. In ancient times they were thought to have magical power. They were the first compasses – the name lodestone meaning "course stone."

Native American Indian flint arrowheads and spear point

## Ancient tools

Humans have been shaping tools and weapons from stone, usually flint, since the Stone Age, some 2.6 million years ago. When flint – a hard, glassy sedimentary rock – is hit, it splits to remove a "flake." Repeated hitting will create sharp edges for an axe, spear, or arrowhead.

## Fact file

### Building materials

Construction uses more of Earth's resources than any industry, and building materials have changed little in over 5,000 years.

**Glass**

First made in 2500 BCE, it is produced by heating sand to over 3,000 °F. Glass can cover buildings from ground to top floor.

**Brick**

Bricks of sand, mud, and water have been in use since 8000 BCE. Yemen's mud brick towers were the world's first skyscrapers.

**Concrete**

Tenerife's Auditorio is built of concrete, which is a mixture of water, gravel, sand, chalk, and clay. It is a relatively new material.

## The greatest wall

The Great Wall of China is the longest wall and largest piece of ancient architecture in the world. The wall is built of granite and kiln-fired bricks, but some sections used rammed earth, limestone and marble. Over one hundred million tons of material was used during its 2,000-years of construction.

The Great Wall of China at Mutianyu is constructed of granite

## Coal power

When coal is burned, the energy in the organic matter (dead plants) is released. This energy can heat water to produce steam that can drive a turbine to generate electricity. Over 40 percent of electricity is produced using coal, releasing excessive carbon dioxide ($CO_2$) into the air.

A coal-fired power plant producing electricity

# Crystals

**Crystals** are solid materials in which the atoms – the building blocks of all matter – are arranged in a regular **pattern**. This pattern is **repeated** over and over again as the crystal grows. At its simplest, a crystal has **flat** surfaces (faces) and sharp edges. The rate at which **magma** cools determines the size of a crystal – rapid **cooling** means small crystals while slow cooling allows large crystals to form. No wonder we find **shiny**, mirror-like crystals fascinating – they are not only **beautiful**, but they are some of Earth's **oldest** and most colorful secrets.

## Facts and figures

**Six crystal shapes**

**Cubic crystals**
Equal sides meet at right angles.
Examples: diamond, pyrite

**Triclinic crystals**
All sides are of different lengths and none meet at right angles.
Examples: turquoise, feldspar

**Orthorhombic crystals**
Similar to monoclinic.
Example: topaz

**Monoclinic crystals**
4 vertical sides not meeting at right angles.
Example: azurite

**Hexagonal crystals**
These have 6 vertical sides meeting at 60 degree angles that are often topped by a 6-sided pyramid.
Example: amethyst

**Tetragonal crystals**
A rectangular prism with square top and bottom.
Example: rutile

## Crystals that melt

Snowflakes are ice crystals that start life as a six-sided crystal prism, but then grow six arms. All ice crystals are unique and most are not perfectly symmetrical.

## Frozen solid

The ancient Greek for crystal, *kystallos*, means icy cold. It was thought that clear quartz was ice frozen so hard it would never melt.

Quartz crystals have six faces topped with a six-sided pyramid

## Did you know?

There is a theory that at the center of the Earth is a crystal of solid iron about the size of our moon. Though temperatures here should melt the iron, extreme pressure prevents it.

**Temperature, pressure, space, and chemical conditions affect crystal growth.**

Blue-green agate microcrystals and white quartz crystals in geodes

## Hidden beauty

Geodes are hollow rocks formed from an air bubble in volcanic rocks or in holes left by decayed plants. The shell around the "hole" hardens and mineral-rich water trickles through, depositing minerals that become tiny microcrystals. These form layers in the geode or grow into larger crystals.

## Oldest crystal

In 2001, a sheep station at Jack Hills, Western Australia, yielded a tiny zircon crystal 4.4 billion years old. It is the earliest sample of the Earth's crust yet discovered. This crystal proves there was water and possibly life on the young planet Earth billions of years ago.

The 4.4 billion-year-old zircon crystal

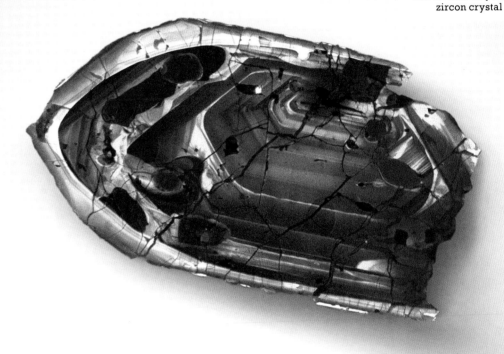

## Edible crystals

Salt crystals are cube shaped (cubic) and sugar crystals and menthol crystals (as used in chewing gum) are six-sided (hexagonal) columns.

## Don't be fooled

Glass is a not a crystal. Even though it can have flat faces and sharp angles, it is a non-crystalline material.

## Giant crystals

Mexico's Cave of Crystals contains 36 ft (11-m) long crystals. Lying almost a mile (1.6 km) underground with a steady 136 °F (58 °C) temperature, the caves provided 500,000 years of perfect crystal-growing conditions. Growth would have continued but the water level was lowered by mistake in 1985.

The amazing Cave of Crystals, Mexico

# Crystal know-how

The internal **structure** of a molecule gives a crystal its shape, color, **texture**, and cleavage (how it splits), plus it determines its hardness and how it **interacts** with light. With the invention of the **scanning** tunneling microscope (STM) in 1981, scientists were finally able to see the individual **atoms** in a crystal and the repeated **pattern** that they form. Naturally-formed crystals are rarely perfect – an atom may be **missing** from the pattern, an **impurity** present, or the temperature changed during crystal formation – but **imperfections** just add to their appeal.

## Facts and figures

**How to identify a crystal**
These are a few of the tests crystallographers use to find out which crystal is which.

**Color**
Identifying by color alone can be unreliable as impurities can affect color and minerals can occur in various colors.

**Cleavage**
Crystals will split along lines of weakness.

**Fluorescence**
Some crystals glow under UV light.

**Hardness**
Mohs Hardness Scale shows the relative hardness of minerals.

**Streak**
The color of the powder produced by a crystal when rubbed on a rough surface.

**Acid test**
How a crystal reacts when treated with acid.

## Crystals are repeated three-dimensional patterns of atoms.

A rare and valuable emerald crystal embedded in a rock containing calcite crystals

## Did you know?

Diamond and graphite (as used in pencils) are both carbon, but graphite atoms are in sheets that slide against each other, and diamond atoms are in an interlocked 3-D lattice.

## Rarest crystal

Painite was for many decades the world's rarest crystal, with only two known samples. Even with recent discoveries, this red gem is still extremely rare and highly sought.

## Crystal experts

Crystallographers study the structure and properties of crystals. Until X-rays were invented, rulers were used to measure crystals!

Butterfly twinned crystals of calcite

## Twinning

When similar crystals grow from a shared point in different directions, it is called twinning. It is caused by an error during crystallization. Quartz, calcite, fluorite, gypsum, and cinnabar are just a few minerals that "twin." Twinned crystals can form various shapes — ones that resemble fishtails, butterflies, and even stars.

## Desert rose

These beautiful formations are found in dry, sandy places where the conditions allow the minerals (gypsum or barite and sand) to form flattened crystals that look like petals. Desert roses are usually 1–3 inches (1.3–10 cm) across, but the largest is 17 in (43 cm).

A fragile gypsum desert rose

## Fact file

### Mohs' scale of hardness

Developed in 1812 by Friedrich Mohs, this test compares the resistance of a mineral when scratched by 10 reference minerals.

**Talc: hardness one**
This is the softest mineral so it will not make a definite groove on any harder minerals. Talc is softer than a fingernail.

**Apatite: hardness five**
This middle-ranking mineral will scratch softer minerals, but leave harder ones unscratched. Glass is harder than apatite.

**Diamond: hardness 10**
This is the hardest of all minerals and will leave a scratch on just about everything other than two very rare substances.

## Spot the difference

It can be difficult to identify these crystals simply by looking at their color and shape. However, testing would show that these two crystals are very different. Topaz and yellow-orange citrine look similar in their natural and cut and polished states, so citrine gemstones are often passed off as the more valuable topaz.

The rare and valuable red-orange topaz

The less valuable citrine

23

# Colorful crystals

**Colorful** crystals are always in demand because they can be cut and **polished** to create beautiful gems. Gems are used to make jewelry or other adornments. Crystals **grown** under perfect conditions have a **consistent** appearance and color and are ideal for turning into **gems**. In nature, though, growing conditions are often less than perfect so a crystal may **lack** color or be flawed. But when a crystal is out of the ground, it can be **artificially** altered to improve it. A colorless **topaz** turns blue when exposed to radiation, and **heat** will make a red ruby a brighter red.

**Of 3,800 minerals, humans only find 100 alluring enough to be gems.**

## Facts and figures

**Birthstones**

Each month is associated with a gem, so many people are given their birthstone as a gift.

**January:** Garnet – friendship and trust.

**February:** Amethyst – peace of mind.

**March:** Bloodstone – cool and calm.

**April:** Diamond – innocence and strength.

**May:** Emerald – loved and happy.

**June:** Agate – health, wealth, and long life.

**July:** Ruby – health, wisdom, wealth, and success in love.

**August:** Sardonyx – love and friendship.

**September:** Sapphire – protected from evil.

**October:** Opal – hope.

**November:** Topaz – having loyal friends.

**December:** Turquoise – protected from evil.

Purple amethyst, citrine and variously colored quartz crystals

## Did you know?

Sapphires can be blue (the most valuable), white, green, yellow, orange, pink, purple, brown, black, colorless, and color changing. A red "sapphire" is a ruby.

## Clear or frosted?

Transparent minerals, like purest diamond, allow light to pass through, much like clear glass. Translucent minerals are like frosted glass, only letting some light through.

## Light blocked

An opaque mineral does not let any light pass through. Lapis lazuli, jet, jadeite, turquoise, and obsidian are opaque gems.

# Quartz

This mineral makes up 12 percent of the Earth's crust and is a compound of silicon and oxygen. Pure quartz is colorless and transparent and its six-sided crystal is topped with a pyramid. Some quartz crystals are large, but those in agate are almost invisible. Sandstone contains quartz.

## Light plays tricks

A crystal get its color from chemicals in its environment, but how we "see" that color is a "trick" of the light. Daylight contains many colors, and when it hits a crystal (or any object), most of the light is absorbed. But the part that is reflected is what we see. If red is reflected, we will see a red crystal.

Large white quartz crystals

## Fact file

### Quartz of many colors

Quartz is the most varied of all minerals and occurs in at least 24 colors and forms. It has been used in jewelry since antiquity.

**Rose quartz**

Varying from light pink to rosy red, its color may come from minerals where it was formed or natural exposure to radiation.

**Smoky quartz**

This gray-brown to almost black quartz can be transparent, translucent, or opaque. Its coloring is due to natural radiation.

**Green quartz**

A green mineral has colored these phantom quartz crystals. A phantom crystal has the outline of a smaller crystal inside.

Red fluorite reflects red light

Green fluorite reflects green light

## Glowing in the dark

About 15 percent of minerals can absorb light and then release light of a different wavelength, which means we see the mineral change color. This is called fluorescence. Minerals can fluoresce up to five colors. If white fluorite is exposed to sunlight and moved to shade, it will glow blue-violet for a few seconds.

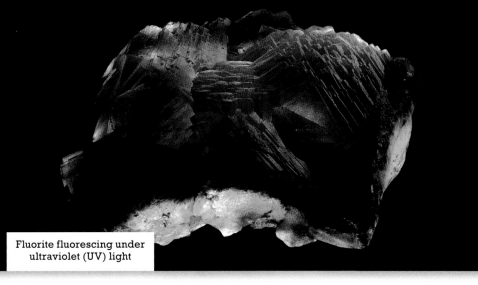

Fluorite fluorescing under ultraviolet (UV) light

# Gems and jewelry

Adorning ourselves with jewelry started over **100,000** years ago when Neanderthals strung eagle talons onto **sinew**. The first "jewels" were stones, shells, **wood**, animal skins, feathers, and bones, which appeared in the ancient societies of Egypt, **India**, and China. They developed the skills to use precious metals and minerals, like **gold**, silver, lapis lazuli, and emerald, and gave them **artistic** and symbolic value. **Jewelry** has always been worn for the same reasons: to show wealth and express **love**. From the first foraged "jewels" grew a large jewelry **industry** worth billions of dollars a year.

## Facts and figures

**Perfect diamond**
The Strawn-Wagner diamond is unique in scoring 0/0/0, indicating no flaws in cut, color, or clarity. It was mined in Arkansas, US, in 1990.

**Most expensive auction jewel**
A pink diamond, known as the Graff Pink, was discovered in the 1950s. It was sold for $46 million, breaking all auction records for a single gem.

**Largest opal**
The Olympic Australis weighs 122 ounces (3,450 grams) and is 99 percent gem quality. It was found in Coober Pedy, South Australia in 1956. It remains uncut.

**Rarest jewel**
Though hotly contested, the Smithsonian Alexandrite, weighing 68.05 carats, is the world's rarest jewel. It changes from green-blue to pink-red under different lighting.

## Gold crystal

Single crystals of gold, silver, and platinum are rare, but in 1914, a single crystal of gold – the size of a golf ball – was found in South America.

## Space gems

Meteorites and impactites (rocks modified by impact with meteorites) can be cut and polished to make gems. These gems that fell from the sky are very rare and valuable.

St. Edward's crown is the oldest and most important piece in the British Crown Jewels

The **Crown Jewels** are **priceless** because of their **history**, not their **gemstones**.

## Did you know?

Since ancient times, gems have been valued for their healing properties. Emerald was believed to cure cholera and malaria, and powdered lapis lazuli was mixed with milk to treat boils.

Red corundum, blue sapphires, and rubies

## Gemstone corundum

This mineral, a compound of aluminum and oxygen, is a ruby in its red form and a sapphire in other colors. The red and blue varieties occur when chromium or iron and titanium are present. These crystals may be heated to improve their color when used as gemstones in jewelry.

## Fact file
### Organic gems

These gems are produced by living organisms or from their decay. Many organic gems are so rare or threatened that their use in jewelry is prohibited.

**Jet**
This black rock is a form of coal. It is made when woody material is buried in sediment, decays, and is then heated.

**Coral**
Coral is formed by tiny organisms that excrete calcium carbonate to form hard white, red, and even black tree-like structures.

**Pearls**
When a grain of sand is trapped in a mollusk's shell, the mollusk covers it in nacre, and layer by layer a natural pearl is formed.

Turban pin (1600s) with emeralds and rubies

An ancient jadeite pendant from Mexico

## Soothing emerald

This green gem has "soothed souls and excited imaginations since antiquity," which is why Egyptian slaves worked in mines to find them for Cleopatra and why the Mogul Mughal Emerald is inscribed with prayer texts. A high-quality emerald is more valuable and desirable than a diamond.

## Non-crystal gems

Gems that have no crystal pattern or set chemical composition are known as mineraloids. Jadeite and opal are mineraloids. Jadeite can be white through to green and even pink. Opals can display a rainbow of colors in each sample, with black opals being the rarest.

A rough opal and a polished opal stone

# Diamonds

Highly valued for their beauty and **durability**, diamonds have come to **symbolize** enduring love. It was long thought that decaying plant matter produced the **carbon** from which diamonds **formed**, but we now know they were formed over 3 billion years ago, long before the appearance of **plants**. Scientists are unsure of how long it takes a **diamond** to grow, but the largest one to survive violent ejection from the Earth is the **Cullinan**. This 137 lb (62 kg) rough diamond was cut to form nine main **gems**. The two largest of these valuable gems are in the **Crown Jewels** in London.

## Facts and figures

**Diamond discoveries**

**400 BCE–1700s**
India is the only producer of diamonds.

**1725**
Diamonds discovered in Brazil, South America.

**1840s**
Diamonds are found in the US.

**1871**
Discovery of the 83.5 carat Star of South Africa in South Africa.

**1908–1967**
Diamonds found in nine other African countries.

**1950s**
Diamonds discovered in Russia and in the gold fields of Australia.

**1991**
Fields found in Canada. The mines are in ice!

**1990s –present**
Global Witness shows that diamonds, called blood diamonds, are funding wars in Africa.

Brilliant round cut diamonds can have 58-facets, or faces

## Did you know?

The blue Hope Diamond, seen here in its latest setting, was mined in the 17th century and has been owned by royalty, stolen, recut, bought, and sold. It is thought to bring bad luck.

## Invincible gemstone

The word diamond comes from the ancient Greek, *adamas*, which means indestructible and invincible. These words describe the extreme hardness of diamonds.

## Grading diamonds

In the 1950s, the 4Cs standard was introduced to grade all diamonds. The 4Cs are color, clarity, cut, and carat.

A natural diamond embedded in a kimberlite rock

## Billions of atoms

When carbon is subjected to temperatures of 1,922 °F (1,050 °C) at depths of 93 miles (150 km) in the Earth's mantle, it will form diamond crystals. It takes billions and billions of carbon atoms to lock together to form a one-carat diamond. The diamonds are brought to the surface in vertical tubes, called kimberlite pipes, in an eruption.

## Types of mining

There are many ways to mine for diamonds, from tunneling underground shafts to searching the earth that was removed from huge holes. Sometimes riverbeds are dug up or seabeds can be drilled for diamonds.

Using explosives to loosen rock in an open cut diamond mine

### Not the real thing

Cubic zirconia is made in a laboratory and, though it looks and sparkles like a diamond, it is much more affordable.

### Natural flaws

The clarity of a diamond relates to the number and types of flaws or marks inside the gem.

# Fewer than one in a million rough diamonds are large enough to produce a one-carat gem.

## Cutting edge

About 70 percent of diamonds are industrial diamonds (bort). These diamonds are not of gem quality. Because of its hardness, diamond is used as an abrasive in cutting and drilling. Diamonds are also used in radiation equipment, lasers, computer disk drives, and electrical circuits.

The diamond-encrusted tip of a dentist's drill

# Crystals at work

Crystals are used in almost every type of modern **technology**. In the 1880s, it was discovered that **crystals** behave in very **predictable** ways when heated, which is what made the "Information Age" possible. The use of crystals in **jewelry** is small in comparison to their **use** in manufacturing, science, and technology. To fulfill the demand, crystals are grown in **laboratories**. A synthetic 32-carat diamond crystal can be **grown** in 300 hours; it would take **billions** of years to form naturally. Crystals have even been grown in the **orbiting** International Space Station!

## Did you know?

Natural crystals often contain impurities, but synthetic crystals can be flawless. Synthetic bismuth crystals grow quickly at the edges, creating an incredible stepped shape.

Electronic circuit boards rely on a crystal vibrating at a precise frequency

**You'll find crystals in salt and sugar, LCD displays, and silicon chips!**

## Crystal navigation

A homing pigeon's great sense of direction may be due to microscopic crystals of magnetite in its beak. These crystals help it navigate using Earth's magnetic fields.

## Kitchen crystals

Bismuth has a low melting point, so synthetic bismuth crystals can be grown in minutes on a household stove!

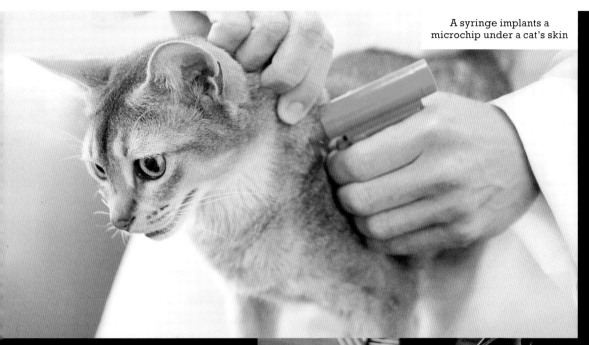

A syringe implants a microchip under a cat's skin

## Tiny microchips

The size of a grain of rice, a microchip is a silicon crystal circuit that can be implanted in people and animals. In medicine, microchip implants can deliver drugs at the right time and quantity to patients. Implanted into a pet, a microchip means a lost pet can be returned to its owner.

## Crystal radio

In the early 20th century, it was discovered that crystalline minerals could be used to pick up radio signals. A crystal detector, connected by a wire, was used in crystal radios. These simple machines heralded the origin of electronics, and today a crystal detector would be called a diode.

A crystal radio with two mineral samples to be used as detectors

### Harder diamonds

Most industrial diamonds are lab-grown, and some are harder than natural diamonds.

### Healing power

The first use of crystals dates back to 400 BCE in ancient Sumeria (now Iraq). The crystals were used in magic potions.

## Synthetic crystals

Laboratory-made crystals are essentially identical to natural crystals. In the melt process, chemicals are dropped through a flame. The melted material collects on a rotating plate and forms a crystal. They can also be made in an autoclave – a steel drum that mimics natural crystal-growing conditions.

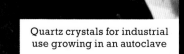

Quartz crystals for industrial use growing in an autoclave

# Glossary

**Aggregate**
Rocks and sediment cemented together.

**Bedrock**
The solid layer of rock under the Earth's uppermost loose surface of soil, clay, gravel, sand, and rock fragments.

**Cave**
A naturally formed chamber in a mountain or cliff on land or in the sea.

**Cleavage**
The shape that occurs when a rock or mineral splits along planes.

**Crystal**
A solid where the smallest particles (atoms) are arranged in a geometrical pattern to form flat faces and sharp angles.

**Earthquake**
Movement of the crust, usually at a fault line, which causes the ground to shake.

**Earth's core**
Two layers at the very center of the Earth make up the core, which is very hot and consists of iron and nickel metals.

**Earth's crust**
This is the outermost layer of solid rock on which we live. It is made up of rocks and minerals.

**Element**
A substance made up of identical atoms. An element is the simplest substance and cannot be broken down.

**Erosion**
The process of moving weathered rock and sediment by wind, water, or ice (glaciers).

**Extrusive rock**
A volcanic rock that cools on the Earth's surface.

**Fault**
A crack in the Earth's crust, often between tectonic plates, which moves over time.

**Fossil**
A fossil is the preserved remains or traces of a living organism from the distant past.

**Geologist**
A scientist who studies the Earth's structure and its history.

**Glacier**
A large, slow-moving body of ice.

**Hardness scale**
The resistance of minerals when they are scratched by another mineral.

**Ice Age**
A period of time in Earth's history of long-term freezing temperatures, resulting in the formation of large sheets of ice.

**Igneous rock**
A rock formed through the cooling of magma or lava.

**Intrusive rock**
Volcanic rock that cools below the Earth's surface.

**Lava**
Lava is molten rock that is expelled to the Earth's surface by a volcano.

**Luster**
How light reflects off a rock or mineral.

**Magma**
Molten rock that is under the Earth's surface.

**Mantle**
This layer lies between the Earth's outer crust and the core. It is made mostly of silicate rocks.

**Metamorphic rock**
A rock that is changed by intense heat and/or pressure into another type of rock.

**Mineral**
A naturally occurring material with a set composition and a uniform structure. A mineral is often a combination of two or more elements.

**Mountain**
A landform that rises above the surrounding land caused by tectonic plates moving toward one another to form volcanoes that erupt or cause uplifts.

**Rock**
A rock is naturally formed when one or more minerals or non-minerals clump together into a solid lump.

**Rock cycle**
The continual process where "new" rocks are made from rocks that already exist.

**Sand**
Loose, medium-fine particles weathered from rocks or minerals.

**Sediment**
Any material that results from weathering and decomposition. It is carried by erosion to bodies of water where it settles on the bottom.

**Sedimentary rock**
Rocks formed when layers of sediment are pressed and cemented together.

**Seismic waves**
Waves of energy released by earthquakes or volcanoes that travel through the Earth.

**Strata**
Layers or bands in rocks.

**Tectonic plates**
Large sections of the Earth's crust that move.

**Volcanic**
Anything caused or created by a volcano.

**Volcano**
An opening in the crust through which molten rock (magma) erupts to the surface as lava.

**Weathering**
The wearing away and breaking down of rocks and landforms, such as cliffs and mountains.

# Index